EV
WITH
JESUS
~
Devotional Collection

STAYING
SPIRITUALLY
FRESH

Two Full Months of Daily Readings by
SELWYN HUGHES

**BROADMAN
& HOLMAN
PUBLISHERS**

Nashville, Tennessee

EVERY DAY WITH JESUS®—STAYING SPIRITUALLY FRESH
Copyright © 2004 by Selwyn Hughes
All rights reserved

Broadman & Holman Publishers
Nashville, Tennessee
ISBN 0-8054-3080-6

Dewey Decimal Classification: 242.64
Subject Heading: DEVOTIONAL LITERATURE

Printed in the United States of America
1 2 3 4 07 06 05 04

Contents

INTRODUCTION

Who of us doesn't long for a life that is filled with joy and effervescent confidence, with each new day stirring within us a reason for rejoicing and expectation?

Long have God's people lived at an unnecessary distance from this reality. Long have they settled for a haphazard experience of God's empowerment and glory. But this need not be the case—not when our Lord and Savior has bathed our souls in His life and newness. What we have received in salvation is able to be renewed over and over again, as His grace which once forgave us becomes ever His grace to sustain us.

In the devotions that follow in this book, you will meet with twelve illuminating insights—many of them well-known yet sadly forgotten in the fast pace and triviality of much of life. These truths touch on all aspects of our personhood—mental, emotional, spiritual, and physical. They find their way into every corner of our common experience. In learning to let God lead us—through these brief reflections and into His ongoing presence—we are daily restored into whole, complete beings who long to love and worship Him.

You will find your life on display throughout this cycle of devotions. Better still, you will discover the biblical pathways to living for Him with daily faithfulness . . . and daily freshness.

FRESH WATER

*"When it empties into the Sea,
the water there becomes fresh."* (47:8)

Our subject is a challenging but deeply inspiring one—
"Staying Spiritually Fresh." The idea for this theme arose out
of a letter I received some time ago which said: "Over the past
year or so, my Christian life has become stale—insufferably so.
I have lost the freshness and spontaneity I once knew. Can you
say something that will help bring back the sparkle into my
Christian experience? What is the remedy?"

I want to introduce you to twelve principles which, when put
into practice, will enable you to maintain spiritual freshness
even though all around you may be stale and arid. These have
worked in my life for over forty years; I believe they will also
work for you.

But can we expect always to live in a state of spiritual alert-
ness and freshness? Isn't that being unrealistically optimistic?
Well, what does Scripture say? It shows us that the people of
God are meant to be beautiful gardens in the midst of a dry
desert. The prophet Isaiah puts it like this: "And you shall be

like a watered garden and like a spring of water whose waters fail not" (Isa. 58:11, AMPLIFIED).

In our text for today, Ezekiel speaks of the river flowing "into the Dead Sea, into the brackish waters which shall turn fresh" (MOFFATT). How thrilling! The river of God flowing into our dead seas turns them fresh. Whatever reasons there are for our lives becoming spiritually stale, it is quite clear from Scripture that they need not be so. God offers to exchange His strength daily for our weakness, His freshness for our staleness.

PRAYER

My Father and my God, I come at the beginning of these meditations to ask that You will make my life like a watered garden. Let Your fresh rivers run into my dead seas so that my whole being is revived—day after day after day. Amen.

FURTHER STUDY

John 4:1-29; 7:37-38; Rev. 7:17
What is the quality of the water that Christ gives?
How did Jesus describe it to the woman?

THE MORNING WATCH

*"Very early in the morning . . . Jesus . . . went off
to a solitary place, where he prayed." (1:35)*

We began the previous reading with the exciting thought that spiritual staleness need not be so. Spiritual freshness is available to us all—and on a daily basis. Maintaining it, however, does not mean that we will be exempted from having to face occasional trials and difficulties. It means, rather, that no matter how dry and difficult our circumstances, our experience of God can remain fresh and vibrant.

What, then, is the first principle of maintaining spiritual freshness? *Establish a daily quiet time with God in order to replenish your spiritual resources.*

Some modern-day Christians balk at this idea. They say, "The Lord is with us all the time. Why do we need to fence off a particular part of the day to spend time with Him? A daily quiet time can soon bring one into legalism." I am well aware of this danger, but again I say—it need not be so. There have been periods in my own life when my quiet time was nothing more than a ritual, but that was more a consequence than a cause.

The best period for a quiet time, in my opinion, is in the morning, before the day starts. Some prefer the evening or per-haps—as in the case of busy mothers and wives—the late morning is better, when the family has left and the house is quiet. Each must establish the best time according to preference or convenience. I'm merely saying that a certain time of the day ought not to *belong* to the day, but to the getting of resources for the day. Start the day right and you will end it right.

PRAYER

O God, help me to see that just as I need to take time out of the day to feed myself physically, so I need to take time out to feed myself spiritually. Help me not just to acknowledge this, but to act on it. In Christ's name I pray. Amen.

FURTHER STUDY

Psa. 119:137–148; 5:1–3; Gen. 28:18; Dan. 6:10
When did the psalmist pray?
When do you pray?

THE STANDARD NOTE

*"Let the morning bring me word of your unfailing love,
for I have put my trust in you." (143:8)*

Jesus felt the need for three simple habits in His earthly life:
(1) He stood up to read; (2) He went up a mountain to pray;
(3) He taught people the Scriptures—all "as His custom was"
(Luke 4:16).

These three habits—reading the Scriptures, exposing oneself
to God in prayer, and passing on to others what one has found
—are basic to the spiritual life. If Jesus Himself couldn't get
along without them, how can we?

I am often asked by interviewers how I maintain my spiritual
life. I usually reply that it centers on a daily quiet time with God.
There are some days when a morning quiet time is not possible,
but most of my mornings begin with a time closeted with God
in prayer.

Someone sent me a brochure once, telling me of a home that
had opened, which they described as "a place in the country
where those who have lost their spiritual freshness may come to
tone up and be invigorated." My quiet time is such a "place."

A sheep rancher in Australia found that his violin was out of tune, and being unable to find another musical instrument to provide him with a standard note, he wrote to a radio station asking them to strike that note. They did just that—stopped a program and struck the note. The sheep rancher caught it, and the violin was in tune again. Your daily quiet time will help you hear God's "standard notes." Then you can tune your flattened notes to His.

PRAYER

O God, I know there is nothing better than I have found in You—except more of what I have found in You. Help me today to catch Your "standard note," and tune every part of my life to it. In Christ's name I ask it. Amen.

FURTHER STUDY

Acts 10:1-8; Luke 6:12; 2 Chron. 29:2
What is recorded of Cornelius?
What is said about Hezekiah?

"CHILDREN OF THE DAWN"

FOR READING AND MEDITATION—

ISAIAH 33:1-24

"O thou Eternal, show us favor . . . be our strong arm, morn after morn." (33:2, MOFFATT)

Those who do not provide for a set-aside time during the day—preferably in the morning, when they can replenish their spiritual resources—may find that they have to provide a time at the end of the day for regret, for repentance, and for eating humble pie.

A traveler in the Himalayas told how he arose very early one morning to watch the sun rise on the towering peaks. He said: "There, as the day began to dawn, we saw arise before our enraptured gaze, within a complete semicircle, twenty peaks each above twenty thousand feet in height, snow-capped with virgin snow. For half an hour the curtain was lifted and we inwardly worshiped. Then the mists began to fill the valleys between, and the view was gone. Gone? No, not really—it was forever laid up in our green and grateful memories."

That is what a quiet time in the early part of the day does for you. Before the mists of worldly happenings blot out your view of God, you can take a time-exposure of Him which is indelibly imprinted on your mind. Then, after the mists close in, the vision is still there within. You live in two worlds at once—drawing physical strength from the world around you while drawing spiritual sustenance from the world above you.

Pascal, the great French philosopher and Christian, once said: "Nearly all the ills of life spring from this simple source: that we are not able to sit still in a room." But what if in the stillness, we were to meet with God? How healing that would be! We would arise with what Stevenson calls "happy morning faces." We would become children of the dawn.

PRAYER

Heavenly Father, give me the wisdom to be able to take "the pause that refreshes," to drink every day from the living Fountain, the Eternal spring. In Jesus' name I pray. Amen.

❧

FURTHER STUDY

Lam. 3:22-26; Psa. 40:1; Isa. 26:8

What was the psalmist's testimony?

What did the psalmist say he would do?

Wait on the Lord *He will help* *Set our feet on the Rock*

ORGANIZING A QUIET TIME

FOR READING AND MEDITATION—

PSALM 62:1-12

*"For God alone my soul waits in silence,
for my hope is from him." (62:5, RSV)*

Someone has described the morning quiet time as "turning the dial until we tune in to God's wavelength—then we get the message." But how do we gain the best results from our quiet time?

First, decide on the amount of time you want to invest in waiting before God. Next, take your Bible and read a portion slowly. Let it soak in. If some words or verses strike you, focus on them in meditation. They will yield up new meanings to you. Write these down.

After the reading, let go, relax, and say to Him: "Father, have You anything to say to me?" Learn to listen. All those who hear God's voice on a regular basis say that it is something they have had to develop over time and by experience. They pause, they wait, and they learn after a while to disentangle their own thoughts from what God is saying.

Then speak to God in prayer. And finally, thank Him for the answer. He always answers—whether it is "yes," "no," or "wait."

His "no" is just as much an answer as His "yes"—sometimes even a better answer.

Not far from my home is the River Thames. Sometimes I walk along the riverbank and watch small boats entering the locks from the adjoining rivers. To get into the Thames, these boats must enter the lock and wait there to be lifted up to a higher level. Our quiet time does that. It shuts us in with God. But then infinite resources begin to bubble up from below, and we are lifted silently and without strain onto a higher level. The lifting is the result of being shut in with God.

PRAYER

O Father, help me resolve to spend a quiet time with You every day. May my quiet time at this moment be the open door through which I glide out onto a higher level of life. In Jesus' name. Amen.

FURTHER STUDY

Psa. 130:1-8; 27:14; 37:7; Isa. 30:18
What do we often find the hardest thing to do?
Take time out today to do this.

SAND IN THE MACHINERY

*"But now you must rid yourselves of . . .
anger, rage, malice, slander and filthy language." (3:8)*

A second thing we must do if we are to maintain spiritual freshness is this: *determine to forgive everyone who hurts us, and refuse to nurse a grudge.* Grudges become glooms.

A few years after World War II, a Christian Japanese boy at a public speaking contest announced that his subject would be "The Sacredness of Work." Some people smiled at his choice, but when they heard his story, their smiles turned to tears. His parents and home were burned to ashes in the atomic bomb explosion at Nagasaki. He was the eldest of three surviving children, and together they knelt in the ashes of their home and prayed to know what to do. One of them said: "I know—we can work." So they set to work, gathering bits of tin and boards, and soon they had built a little hut in which to live. They could have nursed their grudge and become gloomy; instead they forgave, forgot, and went to work.

No one who wants to maintain spiritual freshness can afford to nurse a grudge. It will poison both spirit and body. As one doctor put it: "Grudges put the whole physical and mental system on a war basis instead of on a peace basis."

Walter Alvarez, who is both a medical doctor and counselor, says: "I often tell patients they cannot afford to carry grudges or maintain hates. Such things can make them ill and tire them out. I once saw a man kill himself inch by inch, simply by thinking of nothing but hatred for a relative who had sued him. Within a year or two he was dead." A grudge or a resentment is sand in the machinery of living.

PRAYER

O Father, teach me how to get the splinters of resentment out of my soul and also out of my body. Help me to decide that it is the oil of love, not the sand of resentments, that shall go into the machinery of my life day by day. Amen.

FURTHER STUDY

Eph. 4:21-32; Rom. 3:14; Heb. 12:15
What should not come out of our mouths?
What are we to do?

"He Burns Me Up"

*"Let us keep the Festival, not with . . . malice and
wickedness, but with sincerity and truth." (5:8)*

Is it true that nursing a grudge can cause physical illness? A
man I knew became enraged over something another Christian
had done to him. I advised him to forgive and forget. He
replied: "But every time I see him, he burns me up." I said:
"That's because you want to burn *him* up, and all you succeed
in doing is burning *yourself* up." I told him about the sadistic
farmer who tied a stick of dynamite to a hawk, lit the fuse, and
then turned the bird loose, expecting it to blow itself up in
mid-air. Instead, the hawk flew into the man's barn, and the
explosion wrecked not only the barn but part of his house also.

He listened, but I could see my words had not gone in. He
could think and talk of nothing else but getting even with his
fellow Christian. His wife told me that his breath became foul,
his appetite left him, his digestion became bad, he suffered loss
of sleep and, after a few months, he dropped down dead.

In case someone says, "But there could have been other reasons for his death," I can tell you that I talked to his doctor,

who was a close personal friend of mine, and he told me that the man had died of an "undrained grudge." Of course, you can't put that on a death certificate, but many doctors know that "undrained grudges" play a major role in creating physical disorders. A missionary suffered a breakdown because of a grudge he had held against his ministry organization for not supplying him with enough money. Apparently, grudges are just as deadly in the godly as the ungodly.

PRAYER

Father, I see so clearly that my hurts harm me even more when I harbor them. Help me not to hold on stubbornly to my wounded pride, but consent for You to lance my inner boils, no matter how much it may hurt. In Jesus' name. Amen.

∾

FURTHER STUDY

1 John 2:1-11; Prov. 10:12; Isa. 59:9-10
What brings us back into darkness?
What is the result of walking in darkness?

GETTING WHAT WE GIVE

*"Do not answer a fool according to his folly,
or you will be like him yourself."* (26:4)

We continue to look at the effect of grudges and resentment on the personality. Karl Menninger says: "I know from clinical experience that in some women, the degree of discomfort both in pregnancy and parturition (childbirth) has been directly proportional to the intensity of their resentment at having to live through this phase of the female role."

Sometimes resentments and grudges can be unconscious. As one doctor put it: "It is very difficult to get people to see that illness is the price they pay for their unconscious resentments toward the very things they protest they love." A woman of sixty-five gave her heart to Christ and said: "I've lived with a stone in my heart ever since my mother said she hated me for stopping her from going to another man. Now this stone has gone. I'm free—for the first time in almost half a century."

A man gave a golf ball the name of someone he disliked and struck it, but the ball went into the rough. Isn't that instructive? If you bear a grudge against anyone, you can neither *see* straight nor *drive* straight. The fact is this—you cannot hurt another person without hurting yourself. As the Chinese put it: "He who spits against the wind spits in his own face." We become the product of the qualities we give out. If we give out evil in return for good, then we become evil; we become the thing we give out. But if we give out good for evil, we become good. So mark this and mark it well—you cannot maintain spiritual freshness while you are bearing a grudge.

PRAYER

Heavenly Father, I see that I cannot be an echo of the treatment people give to me. I must echo You and treat people as You treat them. But I cannot do this except by Your grace. I receive that grace now. In Jesus' name I pray. Amen.

FURTHER STUDY

Rom. 12:1-17; Lev. 19:18; Prov. 20:22

What are we not to do?

What are we not to say?

THE CORRODED SOUL

*"Do not let the sun go down
while you are still angry." (4:26)*

We continue meditating on the truth that grudges are sand in the machinery of life. We cannot maintain our spiritual freshness if resentment is allowed to fester in our hearts.

The Christian faith makes it quite clear that whatever shuts out our brother or sister also shuts out our Father. Look at the orders given to us by our Lord: "So if when you are offering your gift at the altar you there remember that your brother has any grievance against you, leave your gift at the altar and go. First make peace with your brother, and then come back and present your gift" (Matt. 5:23-24, AMPLIFIED). Jesus says that religious observance is useless if we are not attempting to be reconciled to our brother, for shutting out our brother shuts out our Father—automatically.

What about when *we* have a grievance against our brother? This: "If your brother sins against you, go and show him his fault, just between the two of you" (Matt. 18:15). Whether we have sinned against our brother or our brother has sinned against us, we are under an obligation to settle it—*as far as we are concerned*. Our brother may not respond, but that is not our responsibility. A Christian must not just go halfway to settle a quarrel with someone; he must go all the way. Whatever shuts out our brother shuts out our Father.

Grudges have no place in a Christian heart. Let the text at the top of the previous page take hold of you today, and don't keep a grudge overnight—for if you do, you will wake up in the morning with a corroded soul.

PRAYER

O God, help me, for I know that grudges and resentments can so blind me that I cannot see straight. Give me grace to relinquish all grudges that are within me—now! For Jesus' sake. Amen.

FURTHER STUDY

Matt. 5:38-48; Prov. 24:29; 1 Pet. 3:9
How are we to repay evil?
How are we to treat our enemies?

LEAVE VENGEANCE TO GOD

FOR READING AND MEDITATION—
LUKE 4:14-30

*"The Spirit of the Lord is on me . . .
to proclaim the year of the Lord's favor." (4:18-19)*

Now and again I stress heavily this matter of grudges, because I have found that this is the truth which always brings a positive response.

Following some remarks I made concerning an unforgiving spirit, a woman wrote: "I had often read in *Every Day with Jesus* your words about forgiveness, and I knew that one day I would have to face up to this challenge. Today's reading demolished all my defenses.

"Intellectually I had always accepted what you said about the need to forgive and that I could not be whole until I had completely forgiven those who had hurt me, but I wouldn't get down to actually putting it into words. I kept holding back my feelings, saying subconsciously: 'I will forgive some day, and then my troubles will be over—but not yet.'

"Your words today came like a bolt from the blue: 'There is usually a reason why we don't want to give up our grudges and resentments. One reason is that we use them to feel sorry for ourselves.' I certainly had done my share of that, but suddenly I let go. It was like a boil bursting. All the pent-up poisons gushed out of me, and I was a new person. I'm in the midst of a campaign now to overcome the misunderstandings of years.'" What happened to this woman can happen now, today, to you. No matter how wronged you have been—forgive.

When Jesus announced His mission in Nazareth, He read from Isaiah's prophecy until He came to the words, "the day of vengeance of our God." Then He closed the book. You do the same. Leave vengeance to God. Use only redemptive goodwill.

PRAYER

Father, help me to realize that nothing anyone has ever done against me compares to what I have done against You. You have forgiven me—help me to forgive others. And not grudgingly, but graciously. In Jesus' name. Amen

FURTHER STUDY

Mark 11:18-25; Luke 11:4; 17:4; Matt. 18:21-22
What are we to do when we pray?
How many times should we forgive?

LEAVE NOTHING BEHIND

FOR READING AND MEDITATION—
ROMANS 6:1-14

*"We died to sin; how can
we live in it any longer?" (6:2)*

We look now at a third thing we must do if we are to stay spiritually fresh: *break decisively with everything of which Christ cannot approve.*

We have seen the importance of getting rid of grudges and resentments, but now we go a stage further and focus on getting rid of everything that mars our relationship with the Master. This means that we must make up our minds that anything the Lord speaks to us about must go. There is to be no trifling with Him.

A gardener who works in an evangelical conference center tells how, during the first two or three days of a conference, Christians are keen to obey the signs that say, "Do not litter." They go out of their way to carry unwanted paper to the litter bins. After four or five days have passed, however, he finds that people grow tired of looking for the bins and hide their unwanted paper under the bushes. They have enough conscience to hide the paper, but not enough to get rid of it.

Do not let this matter of getting rid of the things of which Christ disapproves end in a compromise or a stalemate. Look down into the hidden recesses where your sins may have been tucked away, and bring them all out—every one. They will plead to be left alone, but bring them all out. Not a thing must be left behind. Don't be content with a conscience that will *hide* sins but not get *rid* of sins. If I had to put into one word the biggest single barrier to maintaining spiritual freshness, it would be *procrastination*. So be decisive—beginning today.

PRAYER

Father, I have put my hand to the plow and I do not intend to look back. This shall be no halfway business. Help me to bring to You everything that needs to be dealt with today. Amen.

FURTHER STUDY

Acts 24:1-25; Jer. 8:20; Heb. 3:7-15
What was Felix's mistake?
What lesson must we learn from the children of Israel?

GET ON THE OFFENSIVE

"If your hand causes you to sin, cut it off." (9:43)

We continue meditating on the importance of breaking decisively with everything of which Christ cannot approve. In the previous reading, we discussed the problem of Christians who hide sins but are not willing to get rid of them. Let there be no illusion about this—no one can maintain their spiritual freshness as long as they allow known sin to remain and take root in their lives.

This matter of spiritual freshness is decided, not by living on the defensive, but by living on the offensive. It involves making definite decisions—decisions such as saying "Yes" to all that Christ offers and saying "No" to all that sin offers.

"Christianity," said someone, "is not a prohibition but a privilege." I would agree with that. But I would add that it does, however, have a prohibition in it. In our text for today, Jesus says that if your "hand" or your "eye" causes you to sin, then do something about it. In other words, do not tolerate anything that cuts across the central purpose of your life. From head to foot, you are to belong to Christ.

The order in these verses is important. The order is hand, foot, eye. The "hand" represents the doing of evil, the "foot" the approach toward evil, and the "eye" the seeing of evil with desire from afar.

What's the message in all this? Quite clearly, the message is that sin must be cut out at every stage. The place to begin, of course, is with the "eye"—the place of desire. Take care of that, and you won't have to worry too much about the "hand" and the "foot."

PRAYER

O Father, teach me how to be a decisive and not a double-minded person—especially in relation to this matter of sin. Show me what things I need to break with in my life, and help me to do it. In Jesus' name. Amen.

FURTHER STUDY

Matt. 16:21-27; Luke 14:26-27; Mark 10:28
What does it mean to "take up our cross"?
What was Peter's declaration?

THE PLACE TO KILL A COBRA

*"The eye is the lamp of the body. If your eyes are good,
your whole body will be full of light." (6:22)*

We said that the most effective place to deal with sin is at the "eye" stage. That may mean the actual seeing of evil with the physical eye, or seeing it in imagination with the mental eye. "The best place to kill a cobra," runs an old Indian proverb, "is in its egg."

Most sin follows on from a failure to kill it at the place of desire—the "eye." When an evil thought comes, try blinking your eyes very rapidly and you will discover that the thought is broken up. It is a voluntary act demanding the attention of the will, and thus draws attention away from the evil thought. Add to this action the simple prayer that Peter prayed when he was about to sink into the waters of the Sea of Galilee: "Lord, save me."

Another thing you can do when a sinful thought or desire invades your mind is to change whatever you are doing in order to focus your attention elsewhere. An old Welsh miner I knew told me many years ago that when he was a young man, he was out walking one day and was attacked with an evil thought. He deliberately picked up a heavy stone and carried it back home. The attention necessary to carry the load made him forget the thought.

These ideas may not work for everyone, but they have certainly worked for some. Another way to deal with an evil thought or desire is to focus your attention on a mental picture of Christ on the cross. It is hard to think of evil and Him at the same time. They are incompatibilities.

PRAYER

O Lord, help me to outmaneuver any sinful thoughts that come into my mind. Give me the kind of mind in which You can be at home. This I ask in Jesus' peerless and precious name. Amen.

FURTHER STUDY

Isa. 33:10-17; Psa. 119:59; Prov. 15:26; Rom. 8:6
What is the result of refusing to contemplate evil?
How will you guard your eyes today?

SIN CAN BE OVERCOME

FOR READING AND MEDITATION—
ROMANS 13:1-14

*"Rather, clothe yourselves with
the Lord Jesus Christ." (13:14)*

Every sin can be overcome. Don't allow yourself to admit to any exception, for if you do, this exception will be the loose bolt that causes the bridge to fall down.

One of the sad things about certain sections of the modern-day church is the moral fatalism that says in regard to one's sin: "But what could I do? I am just a frail human being." The implication is that sin is an integral part of human nature, and as long as we remain human, we shall never be able to overcome sin. The clear message of the gospel is spelled out in this verse: "Sin will have no dominion over you." (Rom. 6:14, RSV).

Today's text in the Amplified Bible reads: "But clothe yourself with the Lord Jesus Christ, the Messiah, and make no provision for indulging the flesh—put a stop to thinking about the evil cravings of your physical nature—to gratify its desires and lusts." Notice the phrase: "make no provision for indulging the flesh." In other words, do not provide for failure; provide for victory. There must be an absoluteness about the whole thing.

There are dangers in pretending we are winning the battle against sin when we are not, or in approaching the whole issue from self-effort. But these dangers, in my opinion, are not as great as mentally providing for sin in our lives. The tyranny of this fatalism—that as long as we are in the flesh, we must expect to sin—must be broken. The Christian life must be lived from the standpoint that we expect not to sin. I repeat: *every sin can be overcome.*

PRAYER

My Father and my God, help me to lay hold on the fact that
Your offer is not simply to help me realize what sin is, but
to release me from it. May I enter more and more into
that glorious deliverance day by day. Amen.

FURTHER STUDY

Rom. 7 & 8; 6:11; John 8:34
What set Paul free?
What is the obligation we have?

"BUT YOUR HEAD IS GONE"

FOR READING AND MEDITATION—
COLOSSIANS 2:6-19

"Christ has utterly wiped out the damning evidence of broken laws." (2:14, PHILLIPS)

We look at one more reading which focuses on the thought that one of the things we must do if we are to stay spiritually fresh is to break decisively with everything that Christ cannot approve.

When we are fighting sin and evil, we are fighting a defeated foe, because Jesus met and conquered every sin on the cross. You will never meet a single sin that has not been defeated by Christ. So if sin is bullying you, do what E. Stanley Jones advised. He said: "When sin intimidates me, I quietly ask it to bend its neck. When it does, I joyfully point to the footprints of the Son of God on its neck. My inferiority complex is gone. I am on the winning side." This language may be picturesque, but the truth is powerful—because of what Christ has accomplished on Calvary, we walk the earth amid conquered foes.

A far-fetched but illustrative story from the ancient battles of Africa tells how a warrior was beheaded during a skirmish, but he fought on even though his head was gone. He succeeded in killing many until someone said, "But your head has gone! You're dead," whereupon he fell down and died. When sin comes against you, point and say: "Look, your head has gone. My Master conquered you on the cross. Begone! You are head-less." Evil fights on, but it is brainless. It depends on prejudices, old habits, and perhaps above all on our lack of decisiveness. So if there are still any sins in your life that need to be dealt with, face them in the assurance that they are conquered foes, and break decisively with everything that Christ cannot approve.

PRAYER

O God, thank You for reminding me that I need not develop an inferiority complex in relation to sin—it is a conquered foe. Help me to accept and enter into the great victory of Calvary. In Christ's powerful name. Amen.

FURTHER STUDY

1 John 1; Prov. 28:13; Acts 3:19
What prevents us from prospering?
How are we to deal with sin?

OUR CHIEF RESOURCE

"Be filled with the Spirit." (5:18)

We continue meditating on the things we must do in order to maintain spiritual freshness. My next suggestion is this: *daily open your being to the presence and power of the Holy Spirit.*

A number of Christians I meet shrink from any talk of the Holy Spirit for fear they will be labelled "charismatic." People sometimes write to me and say: "We can't quite tell from your writings whether you are a charismatic or a non-charismatic. What line do you take as far as this is concerned?"

My usual reply is that I refuse to wear any label other than that of a child of the living God. I know that whenever I talk about the Holy Spirit, I run the risk of alienating some of my audience who think that because of the overemphasis in some circles on matters relating to the third Person of the Trinity, it is best to avoid any mention of Him altogether.

According to Scripture, however, the Holy Spirit is the chief resource for spiritual freshness. Unless we have a continuous encounter with Him, our lives will lack vitality and exuberance. I say "continuous encounter," because there are some Christians who think that because they have been filled with the Holy Spirit at some time in their past, that is enough. It is not. Our text for today tells us: "Ever be filled and stimulated with the Holy Spirit" (AMPLIFIED). We need a constant replenishing of the resources of the Holy Spirit. As Billy Graham replied when someone asked why he said he prayed to be continually filled with the Holy Spirit—he answered: "Because I leak."

PRAYER

Gracious Father, fill me with Your Spirit. Help me to know the experience of a daily infilling, a constant topping-up. Help me to be open to all Your resources, especially those that are supplied by Your Spirit. Amen.

FURTHER STUDY

Acts 2; 1:8; Joel 2:28
What did Jesus promise?
What was the result?

WHAT IF?

"But you will receive power when the Holy Spirit comes on you; and you will be my witnesses." (1:8)

A little boy, when asked what the Holy Spirit meant, replied: "I suppose it is what puts the 'oomph' into Christianity." He was on the right track, but failed to use the correct pronoun— not "it" but "He." The Holy Spirit is not an influence but a Person. This is why Scripture, when referring to Him, uses personal pronouns such as "He," "who," and "whom."

Suppose there had been no Holy Spirit? Then we would have been faced with a religion in which there was little "oomph." We would have the four Gospels without the Upper Room— distinctive, but not dynamic.

Take Mark's Gospel, for example. If there had been no day of Pentecost, if the promised Holy Spirit had not been poured out upon God's people, the message of Christ would have ended with these words: "Then they went out and fled from the tomb, for trembling and bewilderment and consternation had seized them. And they said nothing about it to anyone, for they were held by alarm and fear" (Mark 16:8, AMPLIFIED).

What a sad plight we would all be in if the message of Christ had ended there. The resurrection had taken place, the whole of the redemptive process was complete, the gladdest news that had ever burst upon human ears was in the possession of the disciples—but "they said nothing about it to anyone, for they were held by alarm and fear." If Christianity had ended there, it would not have been a gospel that conquered the world. No amount of good information could have transformed those early disciples. Something else was needed—the Holy Spirit.

PRAYER

O God, help me not to live in the twilight zone between Resurrection and Pentecost. I want to know all the fullness of the Upper Room in my life. Turn me from a flickering torch into a flaming torch. In Jesus' name. Amen.

FURTHER STUDY

John 16:1-16; 14:26; 15:26-27
What did Jesus say of the Holy Spirit?
What is another title of the Holy Spirit?

THE DIVIDING LINE

FOR READING AND MEDITATION—

PSALM 5:1-12

"And they were all filled with the Holy Spirit and begin to speak with other tongues." (2:4, NASB)

We ended the previous reading with the thought that it was the Holy Spirit who transformed the early disciples from timid and disconsolate men into ones who were ablaze and invincible.

If you draw a line through the pages of the New Testament, you will find on one side a good deal of spiritual staleness, while on the other an abundance of spiritual freshness. That line runs straight through an Upper Room where a group of people waited in simple confidence for the promise their Master had made to them to be fulfilled. We read: "They were all filled with the Holy Spirit." That filling was the dividing line in the moral and spiritual development of humanity. It marked a new era—the era of the Holy Spirit.

On the other side of that dividing line, prior to Pentecost, the disciples were spasmodic in their allegiance and achievements. Sometimes they could rejoice that evil spirits were subject to them, and sometimes they had to ask, "Why could we not cast it out?" Sometimes they appeared ready to go to death with Jesus, and sometimes they quarrelled over who should have first place in His kingdom. Simon Peter could whip out a sword and cut off the ear of the high priest's servant, and then quail before the gaze of a serving maid.

Then came Pentecost. A divine reinforcement took place. They were new men doing new work—no longer spasmodic, but stable. On which side of that dividing line are you? Are you a pre-Pentecost Christian, spasmodic and intermittent, or a post-Pentecost Christian—dynamic and different?

PRAYER

O God, forgive me that so often I am crouching behind closed doors instead of being out on the open road. Make me a post-Pentecost Christian. In Jesus' name. Amen.

FURTHER STUDY

2 Cor. 3:1-6; John 6:63; Rom. 8:11; 1 Pet. 3:18
What does the letter of the law do?
What changes this?

"LIFE UNLIMITED"

FOR READING AND MEDITATION—
JOHN 7:25-39

"He who believes in Me . . . 'From his innermost being shall flow rivers of living water.'" (7:38, NASB)

It is quite clear from the words before us from John 7:38 that the followers of Christ are meant to have "rivers of living water" flowing out of them. The Amplified Bible translates this passage: "He who believes in Me . . . From his innermost being shall flow continuously springs and rivers of living water. But He was speaking here of the Spirit, Whom those who believe in Him were afterwards to receive."

Are our lives truly like this? Do fresh springs flow out of us day after day? If not, why not? The answer is simple—there can be no outflow unless there is an inflow. This is the rhythm of the Holy Spirit—intake and outflow. If there is more intake than outflow, then the intake stops; if there is more outflow than intake, then the outflow stops. The doors open inward to receive, only to open outward to give.

When we come to talk about life in the Spirit, we are not to think in terms of a reservoir which has only limited resources. Life is a channel, attached to infinite resources. The more we draw on these resources, the more we have. There is no danger of exhausting one's resources. We do not have to hold back—for the more we give, the more we have.

Living on the overflow is what many of us lack today. A sign could be put up over our individual and collective lives saying, "Life Limited." According to Jesus' promise, however, when the Spirit comes, life is *unlimited*: "From your innermost being shall flow rivers of living water." Not rivulets, not trickles, not brooks, not streams—but rivers. Rivers!

PRAYER

O God, take me from "Life Limited" to "Life Unlimited."
Help me to link my channel to Your infinite resources.
Flow through me until I become a flowing river—
no, an overflowing river. In Jesus' name. Amen.

FURTHER STUDY

Acts 10:34-38; 1 Cor. 3:16; 6:19; 2 Tim. 1:14
How did Peter link Christ's work with that of the Spirit?
What has God made us?

THE ABIDING PRESENCE

*"You know Him because He abides with you,
and will be in you." (14:17, NASB)*

There is an all-at-onceness about the coming of the Holy Spirit into our lives—and also a continuity.

Marriage is perhaps the best illustration I can use to clarify what I mean here. Just as there is an all-at-onceness about marriage—you don't get married again every day if you are really married; it is a once and for all—yet there are daily adjustments to be made around this great central adjustment. You can be married all at once, yet it takes a long time to be married well, for more and more mutual adjustments have to be made, and more and more areas of surrender experienced.

"Surrender" is the initial word in any relationship—whether human or divine—and then other words come in, such as "gladly yielding" and "joyful response." As someone has put it: "I surrender to surrender. I yield to yielding. And I respond to response." The initial surrender to God brings, or should bring, an attitude of response to all of God's commands. And one of those commands, remember, is to be continuously filled with the Holy Spirit. As D. L. Moody once put it: "Ephesians 5:18 is not just an experience to be enjoyed but a command to be obeyed. If we do not open ourselves to a daily encounter with the Holy Spirit, the inevitable conclusion is that we are disobedient Christians."

One final word of advice: make sure, when you ask God to fill you daily with His Spirit, that you are not just looking for a momentary thrill or a passing influence that will pull you out of a spiritual "low." He wants to come in—to abide.

PRAYER

O Father, forgive me that I tend to treat the Holy Spirit more as a Visitor than as a Companion. From today on, I want that to change. Come in, Holy Spirit, to reside and preside. In Christ's name I pray. Amen.

FURTHER STUDY

Acts 10:39-48; Judges 6:34; 14:6; 1 Sam. 10:10; 16:13
List some of the O.T. saints who were anointed by the Spirit.
What change did Pentecost make?

A TEMPLE, NOT A TRAP

"A body you prepared for me." (10:5)

~

We continue to meditate on things we must do if we are to stay spiritually fresh. My next suggestion may come as a surprise: *keep your body in good physical shape.*

One of the most disastrous divorces that ever took place in Christendom was that between the physical and the spiritual. In the early days of Christianity, the two were one. When the disciples wanted men to look after the physical nourishment of those who were in need in the early church, the first of those they selected was Stephen, a man "full of faith and of the Holy Spirit" (Acts 6:5, NASB). This combination of faith and the Holy Spirit was to be carried into the satisfying of physical needs, for the early church regarded the physical as being important as well as the spiritual. Not *supremely* important, of course, but important nevertheless.

In more recent centuries, the physical has been looked upon with greater suspicion in the church. In my youth I heard thundering sermons on the text, "our vile body" (Phil. 3:21, KJV), in which preachers propounded the idea that the body was the enemy of the soul. The suggestion was that the body must be ignored until the day when it is finally discarded and we are given a new resurrection body. These preachers failed to understand that the phrase "vile body" in the King James Version really means "body of humiliation," and not something to be treated with contempt. Let's have done with this morbid idea concerning the body which still lingers in parts of the Christian church. Our bodies are not to be seen as traps, but as temples of the Holy Spirit.

PRAYER

Blessed Lord Jesus, help me see my body in the way You saw Yours—not as something to be avoided but as something to be used. Show me the steps I need to take to be healthy in soul and in body. For Your own dear name's sake. Amen.

FURTHER STUDY

Rom. 12:1-8; 6:13; 2 Cor. 6:16
What are we to offer God?
What are we to honor God with?

BODY AND SOUL—UNITED

"May your whole spirit, soul and body be kept blameless at the coming of our Lord Jesus Christ." (5:23)

Many centuries of misunderstanding have brought about a division between body and soul. This division is in evidence in some parts of the church today. Jesus, however, did not see His body as something to be ignored but as something to be used. As He said, "You have made ready a body for Me to offer" (Heb. 10:5, AMPLIFIED).

His body and soul were attuned. He neither neglected His body nor pampered it, but offered it as the vehicle of God's will and purpose. And He kept it fit for God. There is no mention of His ever being sick. Tired, yes, but never ill.

It is accepted today that body and soul are a unity, that a sick soul can produce a sick body, just as a healthy spirit contributes to a healthy body. It also works the other way around—a healthy body can contribute to good emotional and mental health. We Christians tend to overemphasize the spiritual side of life while underestimating the importance of physical facts like body chemistry, weather, water, air pollution, and nutrition.

But through ignorance of the way in which body and soul are related, we succeed only in tearing them apart. I believe what is said about husband and wife in the marriage service can also be applied to the body and the soul: "What therefore God has joined together, let not man put asunder" (Matt. 19:6, RSV).

A good pianist may be able to get a lot out of a poor instrument, but he cannot give full expression to the music if the piano is out of tune. You cannot ignore the physical if you want to stay spiritually fresh.

PRAYER

O Father, help me see that my body is not something over which to be offended, but something to be offered. Give me a balanced understanding of this matter so that I can be at my best for You—spirit, soul, and body. Amen.

FURTHER STUDY

1 Kings 19; Rom. 8:11; 1 Cor. 3:16
What was part of Elijah's problem?
How did the angel minister to Elijah?

DEADLY WEAPONS

*"So whether you eat or drink or whatever you do,
do it all for the glory of God." (10:31)*

Disregard for the physical aspect of life can greatly contribute to spiritual dryness. This means that a certain amount
of discipline must be introduced into our lives. But what kind
of discipline?

Firstly, we need discipline in what and how much we eat.
Every meal should be a sacrament offered on the altar of fitter
and finer living. Doctors tell us that excess food—as well as too
little food—destroys brain power. What is in the stomach often
determines what is in the head. Scripture says, "The kingdom
of God is not food and drink" (Rom. 14:17, NKJV). But it is
not a contradiction of that verse to say that often our food and
drink determine our fitness for the kingdom of God.

Seneca, in an exaggerated statement made for the sake of
emphasis, said, "Man does not die: he kills himself." Dr. R. L.
Greene, a professor of chemistry and a specialist in nutrition,
says, "The most deadly weapons used by man in committing
suicide are the knife, fork, and spoon." You may be repelled at

the idea of committing suicide—and so you should be—but you may well be contributing to your death by choosing wrong ways of eating.

We need discipline also to ensure that we get at least the minimum amount of vitamins. Vitamins are necessary to vitality; they are God's gift to us. The divine Chemist has designed our bodies to work in a certain way. And if we ignore His prescription for health, we reduce our physical effectiveness, which can also reduce our spiritual effectiveness.

PRAYER

O Father, help me recognize that physical vitality contributes to spiritual vitality. May I respect the body You have given me and pay attention to the laws of health that You have built into the universe. In Jesus' name I pray. Amen.

FURTHER STUDY

Prov. 23:1-21; Eccl. 6:7; Phil. 3:19
How does the Scripture regard gluttony?
What is gluttony?

LIKE A FINE-TUNED VIOLIN

FOR READING AND MEDITATION—
I KINGS 19:1-8

"So he got up and ate and drank. Strengthened by that food . . . forty days and forty nights." (19:8)

We saw in the previous reading that what and how much we eat can greatly affect the way we feel. If the nerves are starved on account of a lack of vitamins, they will kick back in physical depression—exactly the same way that a starved soul or spirit will kick back in psychological depression. So discipline yourself to eat correctly and nutritionally.

Next, discipline yourself to take appropriate physical exercise. God designed our bodies for movement, and if they don't move, they get sluggish. Then what happens? A sluggish body contributes to a sluggish spirit.

Time and time again, when counselling people who are suffering with depression, I have recommended (along with other suggestions) that they take up physical exercise. One should not, of course, embark upon vigorous exercise, like playing squash or jogging, without having a medical check-up. But I have been surprised at how even a short, brisk walk can do wonders for the soul.

I feel a word of caution may be needed here, because many people in our culture are fast becoming exercise "freaks." It is possible to regulate the body too much! You should get enough exercise to remain fit, but also keep in mind that too much attention to exercise or sports may drain higher interests. Everything must be kept in balance: just enough food to keep you fit and not enough to make you fat; just enough sleep to keep you fresh and a little less than that which would make you lazy. We must keep our bodies like a fine-tuned violin, and then the music of God will come out from every fiber of our being.

PRAYER

O God of my mind and my body, I come to You to have both of these brought under the control of Your redemption and Your guidance. May I pass on the health of my mind to my body, and the health of my body to my mind. Amen.

FURTHER STUDY

Phil. 3:1-16; 1 Cor. 9:24; Gal. 2:2; Heb. 12:1
What picture did Paul use in illustrating truth?
How much exercise do you take?

BE SELECTIVE

FOR READING AND MEDITATION—
MARK 6:30-44

*"He said to them, 'Come with me by yourselves
to a quiet place and get some rest." (6:31)*

We have been saying over these past few devotions that dis-regard of our physical life may affect our spiritual well-being, for what goes on in the body greatly influences, though it does not control, what goes on in the soul and spirit.

My third suggestion in relation to this physical aspect of our lives is this: discipline your times of rest and recreation.

Some recreations do not recreate; rather, they exhaust one. They leave one morally and spiritually flabby and unfit. I find that after watching some television programs, I have been chal-lenged or lifted, but others leave me feeling inwardly ravished. The delicacies of life seem somehow to have been invaded, the finest flowers of the spirit trampled on, and one comes out drooping. I am learning to be more selective in my recreations. One should never expose oneself to a film or television pro-gram that is likely to leave one spiritually or morally depleted— not if you value the higher values. It is like allowing pigs into your parlor.

The same can be said of other recreations. Some pieces of literature can leave you with a sense of moral and spiritual exhaustion. Don't fall for the idea that one has to read everything that comes to hand in order to understand life. This is where many of our Christian young people need help. Does one have to wallow in a mud-hole in order to understand filth? Does a doctor have to take germs into his own body in order to understand how they function? Recreation is extremely important to help us stay spiritually fresh, but we need to make sure our recreations really recreate.

PRAYER

Father, You have made me for health and rhythm.
Help me to be sensitive to all the things I need to do so that
I am at my best spiritually and physically. I want to honor
You in everything I do—even in my recreations. Amen.

FURTHER STUDY

Heb. 4:1-11; Ex. 33:14; Matt. 11:29
What are we invited to enter into?
What does this mean in practical terms?

OVERCOMING FRUSTRATION

FOR READING AND MEDITATION—
2 CORINTHIANS 10:1-14

*"I take every project prisoner to
make it obey Christ."* (10:5, MOFFATT)

We continue looking at things we can do to stay spiritually fresh. A sixth suggestion is this: *learn how to deal with frustration.* Time and time again, I have sat with people who have said: "What's wrong with me? I feel so low spiritually. I am not involved in sin. Why does my Christian life feel so stale?" On many of these occasions, I have observed that the problem contributing to their feelings of spiritual staleness was an inability to cope with frustration.

One of the most radiant Christians I have ever met was a seed salesman in West Wales whose name was Mordecai Price. Crippled in both his lower limbs by poliomyelitis, he drove a hand-controlled car and would make his way to outlying farms to sell seed to the farmers. Sometimes it would take him an hour just to get out of his car and open a farm gate—but he persevered nevertheless.

One day I said to him: "Don't you get frustrated by your condition? How do you keep going like this when many others would have settled for a lifetime of invalidism and inactivity?" My friend has gone to be with the Lord now, but his reply has lived on in my heart for over thirty years: "I take every project prisoner to make it obey Christ—even the project of poliomyelitis." He had learned how to make his frustration fruitful. When you and I can learn how to turn the ugly into the beautiful, and the evil into the good, then frustration will never get a hold on us. The secret of living is the secret of using. Learn this, and you will never be frustrated again.

PRAYER

O Father, teach me how to turn the ugly into the beautiful, the evil into the good, and take every project prisoner for Christ. I ask this for Your own dear name's sake. Amen.

FURTHER STUDY

2 Cor. 4:1-10; Psa. 44:5; Rom. 8:35-37

What was Paul's testimony?

What does it mean to be "more than a conqueror"?

WHAT IS FRUSTRATION?

FOR READING AND MEDITATION—
2 CORINTHIANS 11:16-30

*"If I must boast, I will boast of the things
that show my weakness." (11:30)*

What is frustration? The dictionary defines it as "being baf-fled, balked, neutralized, disappointed." Is there a strategy that will enable us to deal effectively with such things so that we can stay spiritually fresh?

When I left college and went into the ministry, I came up against so many problems that I became increasingly frustrated. I knew all the theories for staying on top spiritually—getting rid of sin, praying and reading the Bible every day, praising the Lord in all things, seeing everything that happens from His point of view, and so on. But these theories I had learned in theological college just didn't seem to work in everyday life. In fact, looking back on those early years, I think I had learned most of the secrets of effective Christian living except one: how to overcome frustration. I remember crying out to God day after day: "O Lord, show me how to avoid being frustrated."

This secret was taught to me by a radiant Christian woman whose life was filled with more potentially frustrating situations than anyone I have ever known. In fact, I said to her one day: "You seem to be a target for everyone. How do you manage to stay so spiritually alive and alert in all this?" She said: "All my days are happy, even when everyone hits the bull's eye. I heal as quickly as they pull the trigger." I said: "Teach me the secrets of responding like this." She did so, and over the next few devotional readings, I will share them with you.

PRAYER

Father, You have taught me many secrets. Teach me this one also. Show me how to take whatever comes and turn it to good. Give me a spirit that bends without breaking. In Jesus' name I pray. Amen.

~

FURTHER STUDY

Acts 16:1-10; Phil. 4:11-12; 1 Tim. 6:6
What was a key in Paul's life?
How did he overcome frustrating circumstances?

THE LYRE PINE

"He causes his sun to rise on the evil and the good, and sends rain on the righteous and the unrighteous." (5:45)

I ended the previous reading with the promise that I would share with you the lessons taught me by a radiant Christian woman on how to overcome frustration. In case of doubt, let me make clear that the woman concerned was not a thick-skinned individual who cared for nothing and nobody, but rather a highly sensitive person who knew how to turn every test into a testimony.

Here is her prescription for overcoming frustration.

Firstly, realize that Christians aren't exempt from facing problems. It is true that Christians are exempted from many self-inflicted pains which non-Christians bring on themselves through wrong attitudes, wrong moral choices, wrong behavior, and so on. But this apart, every Christian is as subject as a non-Christian to accidents, sickness, and even death. Some years ago a plane full of non-Christian Indian seamen crashed into the Alps; a few days later, fifty-eight Christians, fresh from a conference, crashed in the same Alps.

Secondly, fix in your mind that the Christian answer is along the line of using whatever comes—justice or injustice, pain or pleasure, compliment or criticism. Ever heard of a lyre pine? The lyre pine is a pine tree whose top is shaped like a harp, with a number of branches forming the top, instead of one straight branch. It is produced, they say, by a calamity such as a storm or a lightning flash striking off the original top. Frustrated, it then puts up a whole series of tops stretched on a more or less horizontal bar. This, too, can happen to us—if we let it. Calamity can turn dullness into music, a lone top into a lyre.

PRAYER

Father, let this truth sink deeply into my spirit
so that I will be able to turn all my lone tops into lyres.
Quicken within me today the sense that with You, I can
overcome everything—including frustration. Amen.

FURTHER STUDY

1 Pet. 1:1-7; 4:12-13; John 16:33; 2 Cor. 4:17; Rom. 5:3
What is the sequence of God's dealings in our lives?
How is this working out in your life?

MAKING SADNESS SING

"But he gives us more grace." (4:6)

We continue with our prescription for overcoming frustration, having already looked at two instructions.

Now—thirdly—expect God to supply you with the strength to transform everything that comes to you, making it contribute to the central purposes for which you live. "Expect God to supply you with strength." That is the secret.

In the Christian life, we get what we expect. You likely have heard the story of the woman who, having heard a sermon on the text "Whosoever shall say unto this mountain, Be thou removed," decided to try out her faith on a mountain near her home. Prior to going to sleep, she looked out of her window and said to the mountain, "Be thou removed." In the morning, as soon as she awoke, she looked out, saw that the mountain was still there, and said woefully: "Just as I expected." Yes, in the Christian life, we get what we expect.

Notice the remainder of the phrase from this line of advice: ". . . strength to transform everything that comes . . ." This is what Jesus did. As the Gospel writer recorded, "And He was withdrawn from them about a stone's throw, and He knelt down and prayed, saying 'Father, if it is Your will, take this cup away from Me; nevertheless not My will, but Yours, be done.' Then an angel appeared to Him from heaven, strengthening Him" (Luke 22:41-43, NKJV). Here, God's answer was not to take away the cup but to supply the strength to turn that bitter cup into a cup of salvation, which He would put to the thirsty lips of humanity. In the midst of your trials, don't whine to be released. Ask rather for the strength to make every sadness sing.

PRAYER

Father, don't ever let me forget this lesson—that if I cannot change my surroundings, I can change my soul. Help me see that if I am not saved from a situation, then I can be saved in the situation. I am deeply thankful. Amen.

FURTHER STUDY

Isa. 40; 41:10; 2 Cor. 12:9
What is promised to those who wait on the Lord?
What was Paul's testimony?

POSITIVE THANKSGIVING

*"Let the peace of Christ rule in your hearts. . . .
And be thankful." (3:15)*

We spend one more day looking at a prescription for overcoming frustration.

Fourthly, look for something good to come out of everything that appears bad. How I wish I could hammer this thought into the mind of every Christian. Nowadays, it is almost second nature with me to look for a positive in every negative, but it was not always so. At one time, whenever anything bad happened to me, I used to say: "Oh no, not again! Just when everything seemed to be going right! Why should this happen to me?" I learned, however, to apply this principle, and I can honestly say it has transformed my life and ministry.

This also means learning to thank God for the good that is emerging, instead of brooding over any loss that has been sustained. This positive thanksgiving will make your heart receptive to God's power. He can do anything with a thankful heart, but He will usually do little or nothing with a complaining, self-pitying heart. It is closed to grace.

Fifthly and finally, find someone who is going through difficult circumstances, and help them find victory. Someone has said, "Sorrow expands the soul for joy." For joy? Yes—the joy of being useful and creative. God uses frustrating circumstances to prune you for fruit-bearing.

And the lessons you have learned will go even deeper as you share them with others. *Expression* deepens *impression*. If you syndicate your sorrows, they will multiply. And if you syndicate your blessings, they too will multiply. Learn this secret, and it will help you stay spiritually on top—no matter what.

PRAYER

O God, help me not to be a whiner but a worshiper.
Help me to cultivate an attitude of thanksgiving in all things—
for I know that all things serve. I pray in Jesus' name. Amen.

FURTHER STUDY

Rom. 8:1-7; Psa. 29:11; Phil. 4:7
What brings life and peace?
What will the peace of God do?

EXPERIENCE AND EXPRESSION

FOR READING AND MEDITATION—

LUKE 24:13-35

"They asked . . . 'Were not our hearts burning within us?' . . . Then the two told what happened." (24:32, 35)

We turn now to look at yet another thing we can do to stay spiritually fresh: *take time to share with others the things that God has shared with us.*

Is the Christian life a kind of secret society between God and me? A solitary thing which I share with no one else? Of course not. It is a law of the spiritual life that whatever is not expressed soon dies. The great Bible expositor, Campbell Morgan, said: "There are two ways to kill the ministry of a preacher; one is to kill his *experience* of God and the other is to kill his *expression* of God." If his experience of God dies, then the effect of that central deadness will spread through all his work. It is like a stream without a source, or an effect without a cause.

This is why Paul said to Timothy: "Take heed to yourself and to your teaching" (I Tim. 4:16, RSV). First to "yourself" and then to your "teaching." Paul said something similar to the Ephesian elders: "Take heed to yourselves and to all the flock" (Acts 20:28, RSV).

But if killing a preacher's *experience* of God dries up his ministry, it is also true that killing his *expression* of God can have the same result. A minister who is restricted or restrained from sharing what God has shown him is like a stream that is blocked. He must find some way of getting through or else he will explode. And what is true of a preacher is true of every Christian. Experience (also known as the intake) and expression (the outflow) are the alternate beats of the true Christian heart.

PRAYER

Father, I see that if either of these two things—experience or expression—grow faint within me, then I will lack spiritual vigor and vitality. Help me to maintain a healthy heartbeat—today and every day. Amen.

FURTHER STUDY

Phil. 2:1-13; Matt. 10:32; Luke 12:8
What are we to do?
Who will you share something with today?

WHEN GOD'S PEOPLE SHARE

FOR READING AND MEDITATION—
2 CORINTHIANS 5:11-21

"We are therefore Christ's ambassadors, as though God were making his appeal through us." (5:20)

We looked before at two important aspects of the Christian life—experience and expression. Both of these aspects are extremely important: if experience gets low, then expression gets low; if expression gets low, then experience gets low.

We focus now on *expression*. If this side of the Christian life is not transformed from a bottled-up, non-contagious type of outflowing, then spiritual staleness is the inevitable result.

Two young men, both fairly new converts, had been listening to a sermon on evangelism. Afterwards, they approached their pastor and said: "We have never shared with anyone the experience we have had in Christ. How do we do it?" He suggested that they could go out, knock on a few doors, and just begin to share their experience of Christ. The next night, in fear and trembling, they knocked on the first door of the street which they had decided to evangelize, and found it to be the home of a well-known lawyer. They were a little nonplussed when they discovered this, and blurted out: "We have come to invite you to join our church." The lawyer said: "A lot of people have asked me to join the church over the years. Haven't you anything better than that to say to me?" They said: "Well, how about committing your life to Jesus Christ?"

The lawyer invited them in, and within an hour had surrendered to Christ. "Now, where are you going next," he said, "because I want to go with you." Before the end of the evening, the lawyer had the joy of witnessing another conversion like his own. Things happen when people share.

PRAYER

O Father, help me to come to such a place in my Christian life
that in every situation where You want someone to pass on
a special word from You, You will hear me say,
"Here am I, Lord—send me." Amen.

FURTHER STUDY

Acts 2; 5:20; 18:9; 22:15
What was the hallmark of the early church?
Witness to someone today.

"ANYONE SAVED LATELY?"

FOR READING AND MEDITATION—
PHILIPPIANS 1:1-11

*"I always pray with joy because of your partnership
in the gospel from the first day until now." (1:4-5)*

We continue meditating on the importance of sharing with
others what God has shared with us. Christianity is not merely
a conception but a contagion. And when the contagion is lost,
the possibility is that the conception may also be lost.

An American pastor, an old friend of mine, says:
"Christianity is catching, and if people are not catching it from
us, then perhaps it's because we do not have a sufficiently viru-
lent case of it." Once when he was in England, we visited
Westminster Abbey. He looked around and asked in loud
tones: "Has anyone been saved here lately?" I said I was not
sure, to which he replied: "If a church is not evangelistic, then
it is not evangelical." He was right, but that didn't stop me from
getting him outside as quickly as possible!

"Nothing is really ours," said C. S. Lewis, "until we share it."
The moment someone else shares our experience of Christ,
then the faith means something more to us. The Amplified
Bible translates the text before us today thus: "I thank my God

for your fellowship—your sympathetic cooperation and contributions and partnership—in advancing the good news from the first day you heard it." From the very first day they stepped into the kingdom of God, they began to contribute to it—to spread it. It was not something they learned; it was instinctive. It was as natural as a baby's cry at birth. Sharing Christ with others is not something we can take or leave; it is something which, if we don't take, we can easily lose. For the *expression* of the faith is the *essence* of the faith.

PRAYER

O Father, help us to be like the converts in the church at Philippi
who, from the moment they saw You, wanted to share You.
We ask in Christ's precious and powerful name. Amen.

FURTHER STUDY

Mark 5:15-20; Acts 1:8; 2 Tim. 1:8
What did Jesus tell the man to do?
What was Paul's admonition to Timothy?

FOUR SIMPLE WORDS

"The woman . . . said to the people, 'Come, see a man who told me everything I ever did.'" (4:28-29)

We ended the previous reading with the thought that in the true Christian heart, sharing is instinctive. What was the instinct of the woman at the well as soon as she had received salvation? It was to share what she had found with others.

What I am saying will cause some people to feel guilty, especially those who do not find it easy to share their faith. It is not that we should go out and accost everyone we meet with the message of salvation, but we do need to be alert for every opportunity and to take advantage of it.

The four words which most succinctly summarize the gospel are each found in the Scripture passage before us today. They are these: "come . . . see . . . go . . . tell." We get a firsthand knowledge—"come and see"—and then the instinctive impulse takes over—"go and tell." And if there is no "go and tell" impulse, then perhaps the "come and see" impulse is not ours, or at least it has ceased to hold a commanding place in our lives.

A woman once wrote to me following something I had written in *Every Day with Jesus* and said: "I had a real experience of God and refused to share it with anyone, so it died." How sad. J. B. Phillips' translation of 2 Corinthians 9:10 is luminous: "He who gives the seed to the sower . . ." See the inference? He gives seed only to the one who uses it—the sower. If we won't use the seed, then we won't get it. Our powers are either dead or dedicated. If they are dedicated, they are alive with God. If they are saved up or conserved, they die.

PRAYER

O Father, I ask not for an experience of You—
I already have that. I ask rather for the courage to share it
with others. Give me some seed today, and help me to sow it
in prepared hearts. For Your own dear name's sake. Amen.

FURTHER STUDY

1 Pet. 3:1-16; Psa. 66:16; Isa. 63:7
What must we always be prepared to do?
How did Isaiah and the psalmist do this?

COMMENDING OUR SAVIOR

*"Then those who feared the LORD
talked often one to another."* (3:16, AMPLIFIED)

We come back now to what we said earlier in this particular section about the importance of sharing Christ with others: experience and expression are the alternate beats of the Christian heart. And if these two things are not in operation, the Christian heart ceases to beat. Then what happens? We settle down to dead forms, dead attitudes, and dead prayers.

This matter of sharing, however, must not be limited only to evangelism. It applies also to sharing with other Christians the things God has shared with us.

If God has shown you something today from His Word, then it is imperative that you share it with another Christian. As we have been saying, nothing is really ours until we share it— the expression will deepen the impression. So in seeking to stay spiritually fresh, discipline yourself to share appropriate issues with your Christian *and* non-Christian friends. Many do not do this. They are disciplined in their quiet time or their study of the Scriptures, but they have never disciplined themselves to share. Someone has defined a Christian as one who says by word or deed: "Let me commend my Savior to you." There is no better definition.

I saw a cartoon in a newspaper which showed a woman putting a garment around the shivering body of a little girl. Behind the woman stood Christ throwing a cloak around *her* shoulders. The title of the cartoon was this: "A proven assembly line." It is indeed. Give out to others, and it will be given to you—pressed down and running over. Especially running over.

PRAYER

Father, I reach up to You with one hand and reach out to those in need with the other. Give me some word or message to pass on to a non-Christian or one of my Christian brothers or sisters this day. In Jesus' name. Amen.

FURTHER STUDY

Jer. 20:1-9; Acts 4:20; 2 Cor. 4:13
What was Jeremiah's confession?
What does believing produce?

FELLOWSHIP

FOR READING AND MEDITATION—
I JOHN 1:1-10

*"And our fellowship is with the Father
and with his Son, Jesus Christ." (1:3)*

Another suggestion to help us stay spiritually fresh is this: *seek fellowship with other Christians.* Daniel Rowlands, a famous Welsh revivalist of a past century, said: "The whole purpose of the Christian message can be summarized in a single word—fellowship."

What did he mean? Today's text spells it out clearly. Listen to it as it appears in the Amplified Bible: "What we have seen and heard, we are also telling you, so that you too may realize and enjoy fellowship as partners and partakers with us. And this fellowship that we have . . . is with the Father and with His Son Jesus Christ, the Messiah." At first, John seems to say that the fellowship is "with us," but he hastens to add that our fellowship "is with the Father and with His Son, Jesus Christ."

Follow me carefully now, for what I am about to say can be easily misunderstood: the person who does not know fellowship with God can never know fellowship with anyone else. It must be noted that I am here using the word "fellowship" in its highest possible sense. The one who does not know fellowship with God will feel, consciously or unconsciously, that he is cut off from the very roots of his being. He will feel like a spiritual orphan. This is why our horizontal relationships—that is, our relationship with ourselves and with others—can never be fully realized until we experience a vertical relationship, a relationship with God. Only when we are reconciled with God do we have the potential for experiencing true fellowship with ourselves and with others.

PRAYER

Father, I see that I cannot experience true fellowship
with myself or with others until I have known it with You.
Help me to deepen my fellowship with You so that I might
deepen it with others. In Jesus' name. Amen.

FURTHER STUDY

Ex. 19:1-22; 20:21; 24:2; 25:22; 33:9
What was the key to Moses' ministry?
What was the effect?

MADE FOR FELLOWSHIP

FOR READING AND MEDITATION—
ACTS 2:37-47

"They devoted themselves to the apostles'
teaching and to the fellowship." (2:42)

I read a passage in a book that said: "We can only get to know ourselves and others to the extent that we tune in to the heartbeat of the universe."

Here is a psychologist, a non-Christian, attempting to put into words one of the greatest truths of Scripture—namely, that it is only as we have fellowship with God that we can experience fellowship with ourselves and others. What a pity he could not see that what he calls "the heartbeat of the universe" is the heart that was broken on the cross.

Isn't it sad that so many philosophers and scientists come so close to seeing the reality that lies behind the universe and yet, for some reason, sidestep the great issue of entering into a personal relationship with God? They struggle to know the secrets of the cosmos, and yet miss the "open secret" of God's revelation through Christ which He laid bare at Calvary. Instead, they try to achieve fellowship through psychological processes that leave the heart estranged.

The astonishing rise in our day of the "group therapy movement" testifies to the need of the human heart for fellowship. Almost every country in the world reports a rapid rise of small groups meeting together to encourage, confront, and stimulate one another toward good emotional health and maturity. The world is waking up to the fact that we are made for fellowship. Oh, if only they could see that fellowship which does not begin with God, does not begin.

PRAYER

Father, I am so thankful for the discovery that fellowship cannot be produced by trying but by trusting. It begins and ends with You. Take me deeper into Your heart that I might take others deeper into mine. For Jesus' sake. Amen.

FURTHER STUDY

1 John 1:1-7; Rom. 1:11-12; 12:5
What is the purpose of fellowship?
Who do you have fellowship with?

A Hole in the Roof

For reading and meditation—
1 John 4:7-21

"For anyone who does not love his brother, whom he has seen, cannot love God, whom he has not seen." (4:20)

The experience we gain in fellowshipping with other Christians ends in a deepening of our fellowship with God. This truth was first brought home to me by Norman Grubb, then director of the Worldwide Evangelistic Crusade, an organization for which I have the highest regard.

I once heard him say: "Imagine that at your birth, you are placed in a house with no doors and windows, and by some miracle you are able to survive and grow into an adult. For twenty years or so, you have not known anyone except yourself. Then one day, God blasts a hole in the roof and reveals Himself to you. You experience daily contact with God through that hole in the roof, and day by day you get to know Him better. Suddenly, for the first time in your life, you hear voices outside your house, voices of people like yourself. You long to make contact with them, but you can't get out because there are no doors and windows. However, as you lean against the walls of the house, you become aware that they are fairly thin; one big push and the walls fall outward. As the walls fall down, so does the roof, and assuming that you escape injury, you move forward to greet the people whose voices you have heard but never seen."

"Now," said Norman Grubb, "when the walls came down, so did the roof. This means that your contact with God is no longer restricted to a hole in the roof. The sky is now the limit! The effort we make to fellowship with others results in an even greater awareness and understanding of God."

PRAYER

Father, can this really be true? Can I know You better because I know my brother better? Your Word suggests so. Help me understand it more clearly. In Jesus' name I pray. Amen.

FURTHER STUDY

1 Pet. 3:1-8; 1 Cor. 1:10; Eph. 4:3
What five things did Peter underline for good fellowship?
What are we to make every effort to do?

TOUCHING THE INTANGIBLE

FOR READING AND MEDITATION—
JOHN 14:1-21

*"On that day you will realize that I am in my Father,
and you are in me, and I am in you." (14:20)*

Truly, in making an effort to go outside of ourselves and relate to others, we receive a wider awareness and a deeper understanding of God. This has been one of the greatest and most exciting discoveries of my life. The more I have given myself to my brothers and sisters in Christ, the greater has been my awareness and understanding of God.

I am not saying that in order to know God, we first have to get to know each other. That would be blatant error. We can know *about* Him through such means as creation, providence, and so on, but we can only *know* Him through His Son Jesus Christ. "No one has seen God at any time. The only begotten Son, who is in the bosom of the Father, He has declared Him" (John 1:18, NKJV). However, once we know Him in this way, our fellowship with Him and our understanding of Him can be deepened by our relationship with others who know Him.

How does this work? The more I have focused on learning to listen—really listen—to my brothers and sisters in Christ, the more I have found that the effort I have made to do this has resulted in a heightening of my ability to listen to God. And the more I have sought to understand the mystery of His dealings in their lives, the more I have come to know the depth and beauty of His character. Although down the years I have come to know Him intimately in prayer, I believe I can say that I know Him even better because I have met Him in others.

PRAYER

O Father, how can I sufficiently thank You for the fellowship we have with one another in Christ. In the tangible I see the Intangible, and through the visible I see the Invisible. I am eternally grateful. Amen.

FURTHER STUDY

Gal. 2:1-20; Col. 1:27; 1 John 3:24
How does God make His riches known?
Are those riches being made known to others through you?

THE MEASURE OF MATURITY

"We saw a man driving out demons in your name and we tried to stop him, because he is not one of us." (9:49)

We spend one last devotion thinking through this important issue of how our fellowship with other Christians heightens our understanding of God and helps us stay spiritually fresh. I have no doubt that my fellowship with other Christians has helped more than words can convey in keeping me spiritually alert and topped up. When for some reason I am not able to fellowship with other Christians, my spiritual life tends to sag. This is one of the laws of the Christian life, and we ignore it to our peril.

Dr. E. Stanley Jones, said, "The measure of our spiritual maturity can be and is measured by the breadth and depth of our capacity and willingness for fellowship." Note the words "capacity" and "willingness." This doesn't mean working at enlarging our circle of fellowship—though for some it may mean that—but that we have the capacity and willingness to do it if God should so lead.

I know there are Christians in churches, fellowships, and denominations whom I will never meet down here on earth, but

I have the capacity and willingness to fellowship with them if God were to make it possible. We are only as mature as our willingness and capacity for fellowship. Therefore, if we cannot or do not want to fellowship with others who are truly Christ's, then we are immature Christians. Churches and denominations have different rules and guidelines in relation to mixing with others of different groups, but as far as individual fellowship is concerned, our basis ought to be this: everyone who belongs to Christ should belong to everyone else who belongs to Christ.

PRAYER

Father, I see that if I shut out my brother, I shut out You, and my life will soon become stale. Help me deepen all the areas of my fellowship—my fellowship with You and my fellowship with others. In Jesus' name. Amen.

FURTHER STUDY

John 13:31-35; Rom. 12:5; 1 Cor. 10:17; Gal. 3:28
What is the greatest testimony of Christ to the world?
To what does Paul liken the body of Christ?

THE GREAT STIMULATOR

FOR READING AND MEDITATION—
PHILIPPIANS 2:1-11
"So by all the stimulus of Christ . . ."
(Phil. 2:1, MOFFATT)

Another thing we can do to remain spiritually vibrant is this: *to be a creative and outgoing person.* It is never too late to acquire this characteristic. We are made in the image of our Creator, and when we cease to be creative, we cease to be.

Kagawa, the famous Japanese Christian, used to refer to Jesus as "the great Stimulator." One day some students asked him why he was so fond of this phrase, and he replied: "Because He stimulates the creative center in each one of us, making us first aware of God, and then aware of the infinite possibilities in God."

When I was at school, I struggled with my studies, and although I passed all my examinations and went to college, my passes were always on the borderline. Then I found Christ as the great Stimulator—and what a change. He stimulated the creative center within me, and He so transformed my attitude toward work that within months, I had moved from near the bottom of my classes to near the top.

When taking a seminar in Birmingham, I met a friend who had recently come to live there. "What do you think of Birmingham?" I said. His reply was: "I have lived here for three months," he said, "and every day I keep seeing new horizons." This is what happens when we stay close to Jesus—every day we keep seeing new horizons. In His company we begin to see farther, feel for people on a wider scale, act more decisively, and live on the growing edge of adventure. Why? Because a creative God gives to His creation the same creative impulses.

PRAYER

O God, stimulate my whole being, I pray, so that every day
I shall see new horizons. Help me never to walk with my eyes
focused on the ground, but with my eyes fixed on You.
For Your own dear name's sake I ask it. Amen.

FURTHER STUDY

John 1:1-18; 1 Cor. 8:6; Col. 1:16
Who is at the center of creation?
What happens if He is the center of our lives?

CREATIVE COMMONPLACE

FOR READING AND MEDITATION—
ACTS 6:1-8

*"They chose Stephen, a man full of faith
and of the Holy Spirit; also Philip." (6:5)*

We continue meditating on the importance of being a creative and outgoing person. No matter what happens to you, or when it happens to you, it is never too late to become creative. Pray as one man did who was on the verge of going insane: "O Jesus, come into my soul, my mind, my body, into every brain cell, and help me to be a contributive person." Jesus did come into every brain cell, and that man is now well and contributing to the kingdom of God in an astonishing way.

I wonder, am I talking today to someone who feels they are caught up in so many routines that they are in the rut? Routines often become (if I might coin a word) "rut"-ines. They make us into grooved, non-creative individuals unless—and this is the point—unless we make the commonplace a creative place. And how do we do that? By the creative spirit we bring to it.

Someone has described Philip the evangelist as "a third-rate man in a second-rate task who did a first-rate job." He was quite different from the Philip who was one of Christ's group of twelve disciples. He didn't have the privilege of having been chosen as one of the apostolic band. He was instead one of "the seven" whose task was "to wait on tables." He might have folded up under these limitations and said: "I am in a rut." Instead, he accepted the commonplace as a consecrated place and gently pushed against the barriers until they broke. His creativity marks him out as one of the greatest characters of the New Testament.

PRAYER

O God, help me to turn all common places into creative places. Give me the attitude of Your servant Philip, who turned a routine task into a redemptive one. In Jesus' name I pray this. Amen.

FURTHER STUDY

Col. 3:1-10; 2 Cor. 5:17; Rom. 12:2

In what image is the new self made?

What are you creating at present?

THE BARRIER SMASHER

"The eye is the lamp of the body. If your eyes are good, your whole body will be full of light." (6:22)

We ended the previous reading by saying that Philip was one of the most creative personalities of the New Testament. He pushed against and broke more barriers than any other man of his time. Look at some of the barriers he broke:

(1) He was what some would describe today as a "layman," and he was especially designated to serve at tables. His official "job description" did not include preaching—the task of the apostles. Listen again to what they had said: "It is not right that we should give up preaching the word of God to serve tables" (Acts 6:2, RSV). Yet Philip preached so effectively that he was the only person in the New Testament to be designated as "the evangelist" (Acts 21:8).

(2) He was the first missionary—the first to preach the gospel beyond Jerusalem. Look at how the Amplified Bible puts the verse before us today: "Philip (the deacon, not the apostle) went down to the city of Samaria and proclaimed the Christ, the Messiah, to them." When the apostles heard of the success

Philip was having, they sent down Peter and John to take over the task of introducing them to the work and ministry of the Holy Spirit.

Does this mean that Philip's ministry came to an end? Certainly not. So open was his heart toward God that an angel visited him and directed him into the desert of Gaza to preach to an Ethiopian eunuch who, according to tradition, carried the message of Christ into Africa. Philip's success was not because he rebelled against the routine into which we was placed, but rather that his creative spirit lifted him above it. The creative can't help but create.

PRAYER

O Father, give me, I pray, a creative mind and a creative spirit so that I shall be able to break through all the barriers that life sets up to hem me in. This I ask in Jesus' name. Amen.

FURTHER STUDY

Phil. 3:1-14; Psa. 92:12; Prov. 4:18
What was Paul's continual attitude?
What is the result of the righteous life?

CREATIVITY IS CONTAGIOUS

For reading and meditation—

Acts 21:1-14

*"He had four unmarried daughters
who prophesied." (21:9)*

We have seen how Philip's creative spirit heightened everything he touched. We find no evidence of spiritual staleness in his life. He was spiritually alert, spiritually alive, and spiritually creative.

Our text today tells us that he had four unmarried daughters who prophesied. We must not, of course, ignore the evident work of the Holy Spirit in the lives of these four women, but we must also recognize their father Philip's creative influence in their lives. We often say, "Like father, like son." Here it was a case of "Like father, like daughters." Creativity is contagious.

When you consider that the society in which these daughters were born and brought up was a male-dominated one, the statement that Philip had "four daughters who prophesied" comes as a surprise. What caused these unmarried women to break the mold in which they found themselves and exercise their prophetic gifts? Popular opinion at the time said that women should remain in the background and take no part in public ministry. It was the Holy Spirit, of course, who inspired them to prophesy, but I think I see some of the marks of Philip's creativity rubbing off on them also.

These young women did not stay at home and lament the fact that they were not married. If they could not be creative on a physical level, they could be creative on a spiritual level. Some of the greatest work in the kingdom of God has been done by the spiritual descendants of the daughters of Philip—single women who have had their creativity blocked on one level, but have released it on another level.

PRAYER

Father, I want to thank You today for the ministry of those in Your kingdom who, while remaining single, have produced great and creative achievements. We appreciate them, but as You have taught us, we give all the honor to You. Amen.

FURTHER STUDY

1 Cor. 7; Matt. 19:12
What does Jesus teach about singleness?
How did Paul reinforce this?

"He Died Climbing"

*"I press on toward the goal to win the prize
for which God has called me heavenwards." (3:14)*

We spend one more moment looking at the importance of being a creative and outgoing person. On the tombstone of an Alpine climber are the words: "He died climbing." That should be on the tombstone of every Christian.

Years ago at a Christian conference, a missionary who was well into middle age overheard someone say about him: "John has just about shot his bolt." The missionary was so shocked that he left the conference to spend several days in prayer. He came out of his prayer time with a renewed vision. And thirty-five years later, he was still telling audiences the story of how, in his early fifties, he had found a new lease of life.

A sign frequently seen on British roads is this: "End of reconstruction." While travelling in my car one day, I saw such a sign and said to a friend who was with me: "Where life is concerned, when you get to the end of reconstruction, you are getting near the end." Life should be a constant process of reconstruction as we allow the Holy Spirit to show us new boundaries to cross, new frontiers to conquer, and new challenges to overcome.

A French philosopher has said: "To exist is to change, to change is to mature, to mature is to go on creating oneself endlessly." I would only add one phrase to that: ". . . to go on creating oneself endlessly—in God." When someone asked a famous architect, then eighty-three, what building he would select as his masterpiece, he replied: "My next one." There is no end to being a Christian, only eternal beginnings. Today can be one of them.

PRAYER

My Lord and my God, help me to push back some frontier today and see some new horizon. Make me sensitive to Your creative impulses that flow through me. And teach me the difference between my impulses and Your own. Amen.

FURTHER STUDY

2 Tim. 4:1-8; 2 Cor. 4:16; Eph. 4:24

What was Paul's testimony?

What are we to put on?

SPIRITUAL DIGESTION

FOR READING AND MEDITATION—
PSALM 1:1-6

*"His delight is in the law of the LORD,
and on his law he meditates day and night." (1:2)*

We come to what must be considered as one of the highest priorities in our list of suggestions on staying spiritually fresh: *cultivate the art of Scripture meditation.*

For some reason, Bible meditation has become a lost art in our day. A survey conducted among Christians in the United States showed that only one in ten thousand knew how to mediate in the Scriptures.

What, then, is the art of Scripture meditation? Is it reading parts of the Bible as slowly as possible so that every word sinks in? No. Is it studying a passage with the aid of a commentary so that one understands exactly what the Scripture is saying? No. Is it memorizing certain texts and recalling them to mind whenever one has a spare moment? No. You can do all of these things and still not know how to meditate.

Andrew Murray describes it as "holding the word of God in your heart and mind until it has affected every area of your life." My own definition is this: meditation is the process by which we place the Word of God into the digestive system of the soul, where it is transformed into faith and spiritual energy.

The psalm before us today paints a picture of amazing freshness and vitality. Listen to it again: "He is like a tree planted by streams of water . . . whose leaf does not wither. Whatever he does prospers." What is the secret of this amazing freshness? It is simple—meditation. To draw from Scripture the inspiration and power we need to stay spiritually fresh, we must do more than read it, study it, or even memorize it—we must meditate on it.

PRAYER

O Father, I want so much to learn the art of meditation. Quicken my desire to hide Your word in my heart so that it becomes the hidden springs of action and determines my character and my conduct. In Jesus' name. Amen.

FURTHER STUDY

Josh. 1:1-9; 24:31
What was God's promise to Joshua?
What was the condition—and the result?

WHY FEAR TO MEDITATE?

"Be still, and know that I am God." (46:10)

In our age of increasing uncertainty, one sure way of staying on top is by the continuous activity of Scripture meditation. Many Christians, however, are afraid of the word "meditation." They view it as something to be practiced by gurus, mystics, or the devotees of Eastern religions. They look askance at those who advocate its usefulness and power in the Christian life.

Scripture meditation in the Christian's life, however, is as different from that practiced in Eastern religions as chalk is from cheese. Those who practice these other faiths advocate *emptying* the mind, while the Bible advocates *filling* it—with the truths of God's holy Word.

David Ray, an American author and pastor of a large church, says: "I, for one, looked with suspicion on any Christian who advocated the practice of meditation. I thought to myself: 'They are out of touch with reality. Give me action and work, lots of work. Let somebody else waste his time by staring at the end of his nose.'" Then somebody introduced him to the principles of Scripture meditation. He was shown how to place a verse of Scripture on the tip of his spiritual tongue and slowly suck from it the refreshment it contained.

The verse he chose as the focus of his meditation was the one before us today: "Be still, and know that I am God." Take this text now and begin to focus on it. Place it on the tip of your spiritual tongue and draw from it hour by hour the spiritual refreshment that it contains. In your spare moments, pull it to the center of your mind and begin to experience the joy of drawing from God's Word the power He has placed within it.

PRAYER

Father, I sense that here I am at the crux of this matter of spiritual freshness. Help me not to miss out on any of the lessons You are trying to teach me at this moment in my life. In Jesus' name. Amen.

FURTHER STUDY

1 Pet. 3:1-4; Job 37:14; Psa. 131:2; Isa. 32:17
What is of great worth?
What advice was given to Job?

THE MEDITATION PROCESS

FOR READING AND MEDITATION—
PROVERBS 12:14-28

"The lazy man does not roast his game." (12:27)

We continue exploring the meaning of Scripture meditation. One of the synonyms for "meditate" is the word "ruminate." Many animals, such as sheep, goats, and cows are ruminant animals. They have stomachs with several compartments—the first of which is called the *rumen*. The way a ruminant animal digests its food is fascinating. First, it literally bolts down its food, and then later regurgitates the food out of its first stomach (the rumen) back into its mouth. This regurgitation process enables the food to be thoroughly digested, whereupon it is absorbed into the animal's bloodstream, so becoming part of its life.

The terms *rumination* and *meditation* are parallel words. When a Christian takes a text or phrase from Scripture and turns it over and over in his mind, the truth that is contained in that Scripture is fed into his spiritual digestive system and soon becomes part of his personality. What happened to the breakfast you ate this morning? Assuming you are reading this after breakfast, the meal you have eaten is now being digested and in

100

due course will be distributed to every part of your body in the form of nourishment and energy.

It is the same with meditation. Just as a ruminant animal gets its nourishment and energy from what it eats by regurgitation, so meditation enables a Christian to extract from Scripture the life and energy to read the Bible, study the Bible, or memorize the Bible. To read the Bible without meditating on it is like chewing one's food without swallowing it.

PRAYER

Father, the more I see the possibilities within mediation, the more I am on fire to develop it. Help me to maintain this enthusiasm, for I know that Satan will do everything he can to dissuade me. In Jesus' name. Amen.

FURTHER STUDY

Psa. 119:1–176
See how many times "meditation" occurs in this psalm.
What did the psalmist meditate on?

"THE SECOND THOUGHT"

FOR READING AND MEDITATION—
PHILIPPIANS 4:4-13
"Let your mind dwell on these things."
(4:8, NASB)

❧

"To get the best out of life," said Pascal, "great matters have to be given a second thought." Meditation is just that—giving biblical truths a second thought. If you have been thinking that the way to get the best out of the Bible is by reading it, studying it, or memorizing it, then I urge you to think again. I have found that the way to get the best out of the Bible is by meditating on it.

Reading, studying, and memorizing the Bible are, in the main, intellectual exercises which bring spiritual results. Meditation is not primarily an intellectual exercise but a devotional exercise, a way by which the Word of God is carried into the spiritual digestive system so that it can be translated into spiritual nourishment and energy.

Be careful that you do not misunderstand me here. I am not saying that reading, studying, and memorizing the Bible are not important spiritual exercises. I strongly advocate them. But—it is possible to do all these things and yet fail to draw from the

Scriptures the spiritual nourishment that God has put within them. This comes largely from meditation.

To ensure that this matter is crystal clear, let's go over it again: meditation is the process by which we take a text, thought, or phrase from the Word of God and roll it around in our mind, passing it backward and forward, letting it go out of conscious thought, bringing it back again into consciousness, prodding it, absorbing it, admiring it over and over again until its inherent power pervades our whole personality. God has gone into His Word, and God has to come out of it. Meditation is the way.

PRAYER

O Father, if great matters need a second thought, then help me to slow down and take time to meditate on the truths that are contained in Your precious Word. For Jesus' sake. Amen.

FURTHER STUDY

Col. 3:1-16; Deut. 6:6; Prov. 4:20-21; Jer. 15:16
What does the word "dwell" mean?
How did Jeremiah put it?

"THE UNSEEN SCULPTOR"

FOR READING AND MEDITATION—
PSALM 39:1-13

"As I meditated, the fire burned." (39:3)

What are the benefits of Scripture meditation? They are beyond telling. Here, however, are just some of the benefits the Bible offers to those of us who will take the time to meditate: (1) success—Joshua 1:8 (2) understanding—Psalm 119:99 (3) the ability to wisely discern between right and wrong—Psalm 119:11.

But the one that is most appropriate to our present theme is the one we looked at earlier in Psalm 1—spiritual freshness. This psalm makes it clear that one of the secrets of staying spiritually fresh is to send one's roots down into the Word of God by meditation.

In my teens I knew a man, a miner by trade, whose spiritual freshness and radiance was responsible for turning many people to Jesus Christ. Just before he died, and in the company of several other Christians, I asked him: "What is the secret of your spiritual freshness? You always seem to be on top of things, always radiant. Tell me how you maintain this inner poise and power." He replied in one word—meditation.

I pressed him for some further thoughts on the subject. This is not a verbatim quotation, but as far as I can remember, this is what he said: "Meditation is letting your heart become the workshop of the unseen Sculptor who chisels in its secret chambers the living forms that contribute to character development and an increasing likeness to Jesus Christ." That old man, now in heaven, was one of the greatest illustrations I have ever known of the spiritual freshness and fruitfulness that comes from meditating on God's Word. His experience can be ours— if we meditate.

PRAYER

O Father, help me to master the art of Scripture meditation, so that through the written Word and by the meditated Word, those around me may see the Living Word. Amen.

FURTHER STUDY

Rom. 10:1-9; Deut. 11:18; Prov. 6:23; 2 Cor. 3:3
What happens when the word is in our hearts?
What was Paul's testimony of the Corinthians?

A CHILDHOOD MOTTO

FOR READING AND MEDITATION—
JOHN 8:28-36

*"So if the Son sets you free,
you will be free indeed." (8:36)*

We continue looking at ways to stay spiritually fresh. Another suggestion is—*examine your life to see that you are not being controlled by hidden agendas.* A "hidden agenda," in the sense I am using this phrase, is a negative experience in your past which is influencing your behavior in the present.

Over the years, I have talked to thousands of Christians who have said to me things like this: "I know I am converted and that there is no sin in my life, but yet I seem to be driven by things in my past that I cannot understand. Can you help me?" I have learned to recognize through such conversations that the fears, the hurts, and the negative experiences of life can sometimes stay inside us to intrude into our lives, even though we are adults. We think we are being controlled by God but really, deep down, we are being controlled by the experiences of the past that have never really been recognized and dealt with.

During my childhood, I was constantly told: "Big boys don't cry." Thus I came to believe that it was unmanly to cry or show emotion. When I became a Christian, there were times when I felt like crying before the Lord, but would not permit myself to do so. There were times, too, when I felt like crying with a Christian brother or sister who was distressed (see Rom. 12:15, RSV—"weep with those who weep"), but again could not do so. I was controlled by a "hidden agenda," a childhood motto that said, "Big boys don't cry." One day I surrendered the whole situation into God's hands and was free.

PRAYER

O Father, I come to You once again to ask for Your help
in setting me free from any negative or wrong influences that
may be holding me in the past. I want to move forward—
not backward. Save me, dear Father. Amen.

FURTHER STUDY

1 Cor. 13:1-11; 14:20; Gal. 4:3
What position did Paul come to?
How does this relate to the rest of 1 Corinthians 13?

"Measure Up"

*"Therefore you are no longer
a slave, but a son." (4:7, NASB)*

What "hidden agendas" are in control of your life? Can you recognize things which are going on inside you which hinder you from experiencing spiritual freshness? Many of you will be aware that there are unhealthy emotional pushes within you that sometimes take you in the direction you do not want to go. You are not the driver—you are being driven.

A minister said that, for forty-nine years, a little childhood motto instilled into him by his parents had been running his life. He said: "For many years I struggled in my Christian life. I was an up-and-down Christian. Outwardly I was successful, but inwardly I was like a yo-yo, bouncing between spiritual highs and lows. Then a flash of insight came to me from the Holy Spirit. I suddenly realized that my life was not really being ruled by love for God, but that a childhood motto which had been drummed into me in my early years had taken over and was controlling me. That childhood motto of mine was this: 'Measure up. The better you do, the more we will love you.'"

The Holy Spirit helped him see his "hidden agenda." He came to realize that these two words, "Measure up"—which had carried over from his childhood—were affecting him in his present relationships, including his relationship with God. He was striving to get God to love him, when the truth was that God already loved him—not so much for what he did (that was part of it) but for who he was. Instead of living by the wonderful news of the gospel, he was living by an unseen agenda—in his case, a childhood motto.

PRAYER

Father, I see how easy it is to be held back from entering into the fullness of Your salvation through some "hidden agenda" that was laid down in my past. Help me now to deal with any such influences in my own life. In Jesus' name. Amen.

FURTHER STUDY

Gal. 5; John 8:32; Rom. 8:2

What sets us free?

What "motto" from the past was affecting the Galatians?

DRIVEN OR LED—WHICH?

FOR READING AND MEDITATION—
ROMANS 8:1-17

*"Those who are led by the Spirit of God
are sons of God." (8:14)*

One of the saddest things I have encountered over the years in which I have been attempting to help Christians overcome their problems is to see how many believers are spiritually tied up from trying to work through a "hidden agenda." Instead of living by the wonderful truths of the gospel, they are controlled by the directives of some childhood experience. Some of them are experts at expounding Scripture, but their lives are dictated by an inner script which interferes with their spiritual growth and prevents them from staying spiritually fresh. They confess Christ but are really ruled by a fear—a negative expectation, a hurt, or a wrong assumption from the past.

Does a "hidden agenda" rule your life? Our text today tells us that the true sons and daughters of God are led and controlled by the Holy Spirit. Does the Holy Spirit lead you, or are you driven by some push from the past? Look again at the childhood motto of the minister we looked at in the previous devotion: "Measure up." The implied message in these words was this—"The better you do, the more you will be loved." For many years he thought his life was controlled by Jesus Christ, but the truth was that a childhood motto had become his god and ruled him like a ruthless dictator. He was serving God out of fear rather than love, working *to be* saved rather than working *because* he was saved. This is not to say, of course, that God does not want us to "measure up," because He does (Rom. 8:28-29). We must see, however, that His love is not conditional on that.

PRAYER

O Father, let the wonder of this glorious truth flow deep into my spirit today. Wrap me around in the conviction that I am loved for who I am, not for what I do. I ask this in and through Your peerless and precious name. Amen.

FURTHER STUDY

John 10:1-11; Gal. 5:18; 1 Pet. 2:21
What is the characteristic of the true shepherd?
What is the characteristic of sheep?

THE ENEMY WITHIN

FOR READING AND MEDITATION—
ROMANS 6:1-14

"For we know that our old self was crucified with him so that the body of sin might be done away with." (6:6)

We continue meditating on the issue of "hidden agendas." One question that often comes up is this: "How is it possible for a truly born-again person to have a 'hidden agenda'? Surely things are cleansed and cleared away when Christ enters a person's heart."

Paul Tournier, in *The Person Reborn*, explains this point in a beautiful way. He says that the Christian experience is like a revolution where a new prince has taken over a country by means of a *coup d'etat*. Among the crowd that acclaim him are the followers of the fallen king who has now been dethroned. For a little while they seem to be the most enthusiastic supporters of the new regime, but their change of heart is not sincere; they are still loyal to the king and secretly plan to undermine the prince's power.

Tournier says this is similar to what happens at conversion— the elements that went into our early development hide themselves at our conversion and share in the victory we feel. But

they have not capitulated, and they may later succeed in sabo-
taging that victory if we do not unmask them. However, the
process of unmasking them sometimes takes time and may even
require the help of a minister or counselor. Even now, after
forty years as a Christian, I sometimes come across a "hidden
agenda" in my own life that needs unmasking. When I do, I
deal with it right away by surrendering it to the Lord and asking Him to render it inoperative in my life. And does He
answer such a prayer? I and thousands of others can testify—
He does!

P R A Y E R

*My Father and my God, I need Your help to identify
any "hidden agendas" that may be operative within me.
Show me what they are and help me to lay them at
Your feet. In Jesus' name I ask it. Amen.*

❧

F U R T H E R   S T U D Y

Rom. 8:12-28; Psa. 139:23-24; Col. 2:20; 1 Pet. 2:24
What are we to do with the help of the Holy Spirit?
Echo the psalmist's prayer today.

KATARGEO

"When I was child . . . I thought as a child; but when I became a man, I put away childish things." (13:11, NKJV)

We spend one last devotional reading on this subject of "hidden agendas." Today we ask ourselves: how do we deal with these pushes from our past which tend to influence and control our present attitudes and reactions?

We must find how and where they began. They come especially from the early formative years of childhood. There we were subjected to influences, ideas, and experiences that helped to shape our expectations and attitudes to life. Many of these influences, ideas, and experiences were good—and this point must not be overlooked—but by the same token, many were bad. These negative things sometimes stay inside us and can become dictating forces in our lives. We need the help of the Holy Spirit to track down some of these hidden agendas, and we then need to deal with them in a mature and adult manner.

How do we do this? Look once again at the verse before us today: "But when I became a man, I put away childish things." The Greek word for "put away" is *katargeo*. It is an extremely strong word, meaning "to put away, to break a hold, finish it off, have done with, render inoperative."

Childhood agendas don't just fall away like the leaves fall off the trees in the autumn; we have to "put them away"—we have to *katargeo* them—and be finished with childish things. If the Holy Spirit has identified any hidden agendas in your life, then bring them to Him now and lay them at His feet. Decide to have done with them. Get out of the passenger seat and into the driving seat. Remember—with God, all things are possible.

PRAYER

O Father, give me the victory over all the enemies that may be within me. Katargeo them—render them inoperative—once and for all. In Jesus' name. Amen.

FURTHER STUDY

Heb. 12:1-13; Isa. 55:7; Eph. 4:22
What are we to throw off?
What does "forsake" mean?

GAZE ON HIS FACE

FOR READING AND MEDITATION—
2 CORINTHIANS 3:7-18

*"But we all . . . beholding . . . the glory of the Lord,
are being transformed into the same image."* (3:18, NASB)

We come now to our final suggestion for staying spiritually
fresh: *keep your eyes fully focused on Jesus.*

Our Lord was the most alert and alive person the world has
ever seen. Never once do we read that He experienced spiritual
staleness or had to confess to being out of touch with heaven.
He was always confident, always assured, always in the right
place, always doing the right thing at the right time. Even after
a period of prolonged fasting in the wilderness when He faced
the fiercest of temptations, He turned—not exhausted and
limp as a wet rag—but "in the power of the Spirit." Here was
spiritual freshness to the nth degree.

Our text today tells us that one of the ways by which we can
become more and more like Christ is to stand with unveiled
faces and continually gaze upon Him. It is a breathtaking con-
cept—and so simple. Yet how profound. Look beyond yourself
to Another, and thus free yourself from self-preoccupation.
Have you noticed how many of the religious cults get their fol-

lowers to concentrate on the divinity within them? Then what happens? They finish up preoccupied with their own states of mind and emotion. As someone put it: "If I worship the divinity within me, I will probably end up worshiping myself."

The verse before us today gets our gaze in the right place—on the face of Christ. The attention we give to this is important, for whatever gets our attention gets *us*. Therefore, when Christ gets our attention, He also gets us. Our gaze must be person-centered, not problem-centered. And that Person must be Jesus Christ.

PRAYER

Blessed Lord Jesus, when I look at myself I feel
unworthy and inadequate. But when I look at You,
I feel anything is possible. Help me not just to glance
at You, but gaze at You—continuously. Amen.

FURTHER STUDY

Rom. 8:29-39; John 1:36; Col. 2:2-3
What is God's plan for us?
What was John's declaration?

THE "REDEEMED LOOK"

"Those who look to him are radiant." (34:5)

In the previous reading we saw the importance of getting our attention focused in the right place. At times it is right to look within ourselves, but we should not spend too much time doing that. Someone put it like this: "If you look long at yourself, you will become discouraged. If you look long at others, you will be distracted. But if you look long at Christ, you will take on His likeness."

We do become like that on which we gaze habitually. I meet many people whose faces look like what they are looking at—nothing. No character shows on their face, just a blur. It reminds me of a prospective customer who walked into a shop and enquired: "Do you keep stationery here?" "No," replied the assistant, "we keep moving." Many in this modern age keep moving not only their bodies but also their focus of attention, and the result is a blurred face.

Then I meet others whose faces show that they are seeing a Face—the face of Jesus. And their faces are not a blur but a blessing. I heard that a beggar once cried out to a Christian:

"You with heaven in your face, please give me a penny."
Nietzsche, the famous philosopher, commented on this idea
when he said: "If the Christians want us to believe in
Christianity, they must look redeemed."

Far too few of us have the redeemed look. But the ones that
do are those whose gaze is centered on Jesus Christ. Have you
ever noticed how a husband and wife who are deeply in love
with one another grow to look like each other? They have
gazed into the limpid depths of each other's souls for so long,
they become like each other in countenance.

PRAYER

Lord Jesus, You have my heart—have my face, too.
Let it look as though it belongs to You. Let the light of Your
countenance lighten my countenance. In Your name. Amen.

FURTHER STUDY

Acts 3:1-16; John 16:24; 1 Pet. 1:8
What was Peter's message?
What should be reflected in our faces?

"To Look at You"

"They saw no one but Jesus only."
(17:8, RSV)

～

When we gaze at Christ's face and make Him the center of our attention and love, then we are gradually and continuously changed into the likeness of Christ. Thus we are transformed from one degree of glory to another, the Spirit within us being the silent Artist who makes us into His image. We become like Him in character and in countenance.

A young man was so much like his father in appearance that it prompted everyone who knew him to comment on the fact. The mother said: "It's strange, because when Andrew was a small child, he looked so much like me. Then, when he was about five, he became intrigued with being with his father. He used to go into his father's study and sit there until his father would say, 'Is there anything you want?' Andrew would reply, 'No, I don't want anything; I just want to look at you.' He would sit there and lovingly gaze into his father's face for such a long time that I honestly believe this is how he has come to look so much like him."

Just as there is a law in photography that says: "The angle of incidence equals the angle of reflection"—in other words, if you want a full-face reproduction, you must look full-face into the camera—so there is a law in life that causes us to become like that on which we gaze. If we look sideways on Christ, we get only a partial reflection. If we look fully at Him, we get a full reflection. We become like that on which we gaze.

PRAYER

*My Lord and my God, forgive me that so often I just
give You a sideways glance when I ought to be continuously
gazing into Your Face. Help me to behold You, so that I am
transformed from what I am into what You are. Amen.*

FURTHER STUDY

Mark 5:1-20; Luke 23:44-49; Matt. 27:55-56
What was the centurion's response?
What did the demoniac do when he saw Jesus?

"THE GLORY"

FOR READING AND MEDITATION—
JAMES 2:1-13

*"As you believe in our Lord Jesus Christ,
who is the Glory . . ."* (2:1, MOFFATT)

Can you think of anything that could occupy our attention more profitably than considering how to become more like Jesus? The central condition of this is the "unveiled face." As the Scripture says, "All of us, as with unveiled face, because we continued to behold as in a mirror the glory of the Lord, are constantly being transfigured into His very own image in ever increasing splendor and from one degree of glory to another" (2 Cor. 3:18, AMPLIFIED).

Notice, however, that we must lift the veils if we are to be transformed. When Jesus was crucified, the veil of the temple was rent in two, symbolising the fact that the heart of the universe was laid bare as redemptive love. Since God has unveiled Himself in Jesus, so we in response ought to unveil our faces, drop our masks, gaze in wonder—and in the gazing, be made like Him. It may be that there will be many veils that you will have to lift—veils of dishonesty, hypocrisy, legalism, pride—but I assure you that when they go, He comes.

Just think—we who are born of the dust of the earth are being gradually transformed into the most beautiful image this planet has ever seen: the image of Christ. What a destiny! The wonder of that transformation can only be explained by one word—"glory." The drabness, staleness, and dullness of life is replaced by living that has freshness in it. Can we live continuously like that? Yes—in His strength. "Grace" and "glory" are often connected in the New Testament. Take the grace, and you get the glory. What a way to live. Glory! Glory! Glory!

PRAYER

Father, help me to lift every veil in my life so that the light of Your countenance may shine through. You are Light and You want to make me light. Let Your radiance steal into every darkened corner of my being now and forever. Amen.

∼

FURTHER STUDY

John 1:10-14; Col. 1:6; 2 Pet. 3:18
What were the characteristics of Christ's glory?
Make them the characteristics of your own life.

OTHER BOOKS IN THIS SERIES

If you've enjoyed your experience with this devotional book, look for more Every Day with Jesus® titles by Selwyn Hughes.

Every Day with Jesus: The Lord's Prayer
0-8054-2735-X

Every Day with Jesus: The Spirit-Filled Life
0-8054-2736-8

Every Day with Jesus: The Character of God
0-8054-2737-6

Every Day with Jesus: Hinds' Feet, High Places
0-8054-3088-I

Every Day with Jesus: The Armor of God
0-8054-3079-2

Every Day with Jesus: Staying Spiritually Fresh
0-8054-3080-6

ALSO BY SELWYN HUGHES

Every Day Light   0-8054-0188-1
with paintings by Thomas Kinkade

Every Day Light: Water for the Soul   0-8054-1774-5
with paintings by Thomas Kinkade

Every Day Light: Light for the Path   0-8054-2143-2
with paintings by Larry Dyke

Every Day Light: Treasure for the Heart   0-8054-2428-8
with paintings by Larry Dyke

Every Day Light Devotional Journal   0-8054-3309-0

Christ Empowered Living   0-8054-2450-4

Cover to Cover   0-8054-2144-0
A Chronological Plan to Read the Bible in One Year

Hope Eternal   0-8054-1767-2

Jesus-The Light of the World   0-8054-2089-4
with paintings by Larry Dyke

The Selwyn Hughes Signature Series
Born to Praise   0-8054-2091-6
Discovering Life's Greatest Purpose   0-8054-2323-0
God: The Enough   0-8054-2372-9
Prayer: The Greatest Power   0-8054-2349-4

Trusted
All Over the World

Daily Devotionals

Books and Videos

Day and Residential Courses

Counselling Training

Biblical Study Courses

Regional Seminars

Ministry to Women

CWR have been providing training and resources for Christians since the 1960s. From our headquarters at Waverley Abbey House we have been serving God's people with a vision to help apply God's Word to everyday life and relationships. The daily devotional *Every Day with Jesus* is read by over three-quarters of a million people in more than 150 countries, and our unique courses in biblical studies and pastoral care are respected all over the world.

For a free brochure about our seminars and courses or a catalogue of CWR resources please contact us at the following address:

CWR,
Waverley Abbey House,
Waverley Lane,
Farnham,
Surrey GU9 8EP

Telephone: 01252 784700
Email: mail@cwr.org.uk
Website: www.cwr.org.uk

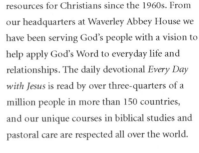